I0817408

Fahrenheit 451

Lightbox Literature Studies

Valerie Weber and Katie Gillespie

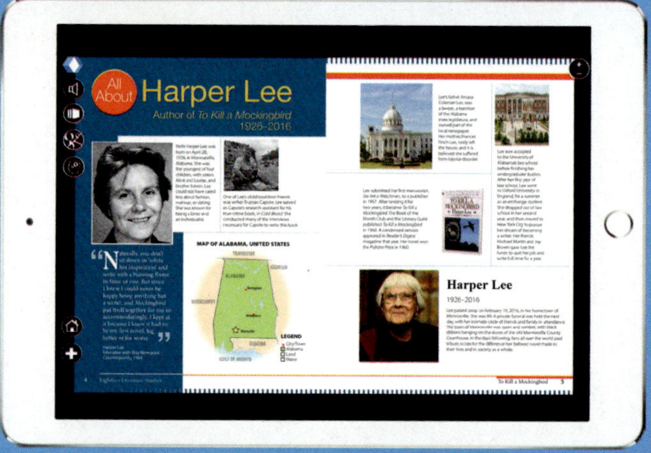

Lightbox is an all-inclusive digital solution for the teaching and learning of curriculum topics in an original, groundbreaking way. Lightbox is based on National Curriculum Standards.

STANDARD FEATURES OF LIGHTBOX

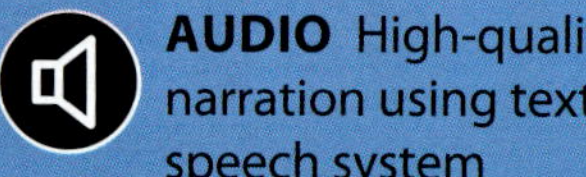

AUDIO High-quality narration using text-to-speech system

VIDEOS Embedded high-definition video clips

ACTIVITIES Printable PDFs that can be emailed and graded

WEBLINKS Curated links to external, child-safe resources

SLIDESHOWS Pictorial overviews of key concepts

TRANSPARENCIES Step-by-step layering of maps, diagrams, charts, and timelines

INTERACTIVE MAPS Interactive maps and aerial satellite imagery

QUIZZES Ten multiple choice questions that are automatically graded and emailed for teacher assessment

KEY WORDS Matching key concepts to their definitions

MORE Extra information and details on the subject

FIRST HAND Letters, diaries, and other primary sources

DOCS Speeches, newspaper articles, and other historical documents

Contents

RUBRIC

Conducting an Interview

Students will conduct an interview with a community member about a time period in their community's history, and submit an audio recording and transcript of the interview. An exemplary interview will meet the following criteria.

- Clearly defines the purpose of the interview
- Conducts thorough background research to inform the focus of the interview and the questions
- Drafts a complete list of thoughtful, in-depth, and varied questions prior to the interview
- Interviews a subject with relevant knowledge on the topic and time period in question
- Asks questions in a logical order, building upon each other
- Treats the interview subject in a polite, respectful, and professional manner
- Does not interrupt or rush the interview subject
- Shows interest and enthusiasm in responses and follow-up questions
- Chooses follow-up questions that demonstrate active listening
- Asks for clarification and further details when necessary
- Asks questions about personal experiences related to the topic
- Asks questions regarding factual information and the interview subject's opinion on the topic
- Asks creative questions that reflect fresh insights on the topic
- Records the full interview in a quiet environment
- Organizes and edits the interview transcript to be clear and factual

Ray Bradbury

Author of *Fahrenheit 451*
1920–2012

Ray Bradbury was born in Waukegan, Illinois, on August 22, 1920. Bradbury's father left the family newspaper business to install telephone lines, and his mother was a Swedish immigrant to Illinois. As a child, Bradbury immersed himself in written material. He especially enjoyed comic strips, science fiction magazines, Frank Baum's *Oz* books, myths, fairy tales, and the stories and poems of Edgar Allen Poe. Bradbury began writing stories about landing on Mars, and received his first toy typewriter at age 12. Like his mother, Bradbury was an avid moviegoer, anxious to see films such as *King Kong*, *Murders in the Wax Museum*, and *The Mummy*. In one of his first jobs, Bradbury read comic strips to children on the radio.

> "*Fahrenheit 451* just came with its own spirit. But now that it's everywhere, I'm so happy that so many people love it. I love that book too. Remember this—I am not a science fiction writer. All of my books are fantasy writings. All my books are fantasies. But the one book that I've written that's pure science fiction is *Fahrenheit 451*."
>
> Ray Bradbury

MAP OF THE UNITED STATES

CANADA
UNITED STATES
MEXICO
Waukegan
Chicago
St. Louis
Glendale
Los Angeles
San Diego
N
E
S
W

SCALE 0 250 miles
250 kilometers

LEGEND

- Featured Location
- California
- Illinois
- Missouri
- Canada/Mexico
- United States
- Water

In 1934, Bradbury's family moved to Los Angeles, California. In high school, Bradbury was active in both the poetry and drama clubs, writing scripts for the annual talent show. Although he could not afford college after high school, Bradbury wrote plays and used the library constantly. He also read a great deal, including works by authors such as John Steinbeck, Ernest Hemingway, Willa Cather, Edith Wharton, and Eudora Welty.

Bradbury self-published his own stories in a **fanzine**. In 1941, at age 21, he sold his first short story, and not long after, he became a full-time writer. Bradbury married in 1947, and his first book, *Dark Carnival*, was published that same year.

Fahrenheit 451 was written in stages, first appearing as the story *Bright Phoenix* in 1947. In 1951, Bradbury combined this with another story and published it as *The Fireman*, a novella which continued the theme of book burning. He wrote *The Fireman* at a rapid pace in the local library on a rented typewriter. Two years later, he expanded the novella into the novel *Fahrenheit 451*.

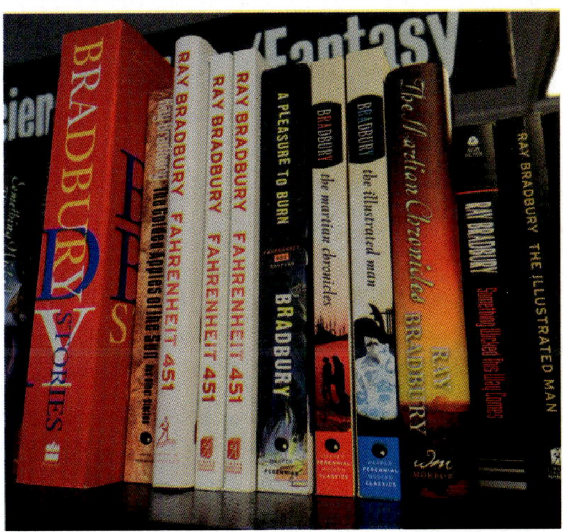

Bradbury spent the rest of his life writing hundreds of works, including short stories, novels, essays, poems, movies, television shows, plays, mysteries, detective novels, and gothic horror pieces. He also advised architects on a concept for the Glendale Galleria, a shopping mall in Glendale, California. In addition to being an executive producer, he also wrote all 65 episodes of *The Ray Bradbury Theater* television show. In 1970, Bradbury appeared at the first Comic-Con International Convention in San Diego, California, and spoke there many times afterward. He was passionate about writing, trying to write 1,000 words each day. Bradbury died in 2012.

ACTIVITIES

Google Maps

Chicago, Illinois

Explore the city where Montag and Mildred first meet in *Fahrenheit 451*, using street view. The city of Chicago is also less than 50 miles (80 kilometers) away from Waukegan, Illinois, where the novel's author, Ray Bradbury, was born.

First Hand

Q&A: Ray Bradbury

Examine this interview with Ray Bradbury from *Time* magazine, published on August 23, 2010.

1. What types of questions does the interviewer ask? What topics does he focus on? Why would he focus on these specific areas?
2. Bradbury says that not reading books is a worse crime than burning them. How is this belief evidenced in *Fahrenheit 451*? Do you think that Montag would agree with this claim? Why or why not? Support your opinion with evidence from the text.

RUBRIC

Researching for a Writing Assignment

Students will complete a thorough research process to prepare for a writing assignment, and organize their research in a logical manner that supports their writing. An exemplary research process will meet the following criteria.

- Creates a goal for the research, based on the topic and working thesis
- Creates specific, thoughtful, and inventive research questions that are relevant to the topic of the writing assignment
- Produces a list of categories, key words, and related ideas to effectively assist in researching
- Uses high-quality sources that pertain to the topic and come in a variety of formats, such as books, journals, primary sources, websites, and databases
- Determines accuracy of all sources
- Uses sources that provide balanced research and various perspectives on the topic in question
- Takes notes to highlight the key facts and ideas in order to answer all research questions
- Extracts relevant, detailed information from the sources during the note-taking process
- Organizes the research notes in a clear and concise manner
- Organizes the research notes logically and in a way that sets up the information and ideas for analysis and the writing process
- Analyzes the information and produces ideas and points to support the working thesis
- Uses an effective and suitable format to present all research
- Properly cites all sources used

Setting of the Novel

Bradbury is purposely vague about the setting of *Fahrenheit 451* and gives only two recognizable locations in the novel. The first is Chicago, where Montag, the main character, met his wife, Mildred. The second location is St. Louis, where Professor Faber can flee to by bus. Through other hints, the reader understands that the book takes place somewhere in North America, likely in the United States. The city is on a river that leads to the countryside. Bradbury deliberately chooses to be imprecise, wanting readers to imagine the events taking place in a city familiar to them. The city is a metaphor for a mindless, pleasure-seeking, self-protective way of life.

Advanced **technology** infuses the setting. Many science fiction writers of the 1940s and 1950s thought of technology as a boon to humans, but Bradbury did not, setting the novel in a future **dystopia** where technology creates distance between people. Much of this technology did not actually exist when Bradbury wrote *Fahrenheit 451*. Called "the father of virtual reality," he predicted a number of inventions that readers are familiar with today. In the novel, flat-screen televisions **sedate** the masses with interactive shows, earbuds allow people to privately screen news, music, and other programming, and robot tellers deal out cash on demand like today's ATMs. Characters are obsessed with this technology. Mildred begs Montag for the money to install a fourth flat-screen television in their parlor, and she loves her high-speed car, using it to distract herself from her life. Killing animals in the process is a side benefit for her.

Snapshot

3.9 million American households had a television set in **1950**. By 1953, when ***Fahrenheit 451*** was published, that number had increased to **20.4 million**.

In **1998**, the **first flat-screen** televisions began selling commercially.

Although French engineer **Ernest Mercadier** patented a set of **in-ear headphones in 1891**, they did not become popular until **2001**, when Apple started selling iPods.

School violence, which was relatively unknown in the 1950s, erupts frequently in the novel. Clarisse, Montag's young friend, tells him that six of her friends had been shot and ten had died in car accidents in the last year. Jet cars speed along highways at up to 130 miles (209 kilometers) per hour, a velocity which creates the need for billboards that are hundreds of feet (meters) long, since drivers and passengers require that much time to absorb their content.

Bradbury creates a world that is not too different from the present, in order to make sure his readers can still relate to his narrative. His characters ride the subway to neighborhoods with trees and sidewalks while advertisements bombard them. They also eat toast, albeit buttered by a machine.

The Fictional City

"He walked out of the fire station and along the midnight street toward the subway where the silent air-propelled train slid soundlessly down its lubricated flue in the earth and let him out with a great puff of warm air onto the cream-tiled escalator rising to the suburb."

Montag, Part One

ACTIVITIES

Video

Fahrenheit 451 by Ray Bradbury | Summary & Analysis

Find out more about *Fahrenheit 451* by watching this video.

1. In the video, it is explained that *Fahrenheit 451* takes place in a fictional world in which the United States is the victor of nuclear wars. Why did Bradbury choose this as the novel's setting? How does this dystopian world affect other elements of the novel? Give examples from the text to support your answer.
2. Why do you think Bradbury does not disclose the specific setting of the novel? What effect does this have? How might the novel be different if Bradbury had identified a particular location as the setting? Explain your answer.

Weblink

Dystopias: Definition and Characteristics

Learn more about dystopian societies in literature.

1. Which characteristics of a dystopian society apply to Fahrenheit 451? Are there any that do not fit the setting of the novel? Give evidence from the text to support your analysis.
2. How well does Montag fit the criteria of a dystopian protagonist? Is this an appropriate label for him? Why or why not?

Time Period of the Novel

Fahrenheit 451 takes place in the future, some time after 1990, but Bradbury does not give an exact year. However, readers do know that the United States has begun and won two atomic wars, and a third war begins toward the end of the book.

The story covers a period of several weeks in the life of Montag. He starts to reject his unthinking life of burning books and his alienated wife. He becomes obsessed with books and the ideas that they contain. Finally, he leaves his job, his life, his wife, and his shattered city behind.

Bradbury wrote *Fahrenheit 451* in reaction to the times in which he grew up and lived. Led by Adolf Hitler, the **Nazis** had taken power in Germany in January 1933. By May, German students inspired by the Nazis began burning books. The authors of those books had expressed views counter to Nazi ideals.

The End of the War

"The bombardment was to all intents and purposes finished once the jets had sighted their target, alerted their bombardier at five thousand miles an hour; as quick as the whisper of a scythe the war was finished. Once the bomb release was yanked, it was over. Now, a full three seconds, all of the time in history, before the bombs struck, the enemy ships themselves were gone half around the visible world..."

Part Three

Bradbury told the story of hearing about Hitler and the bonfires of books. Bradbury explained how after that, "I learned about the libraries in Alexandria burning five thousand years ago. That grieved my soul. Since I'm self-educated, that means my educators—the libraries—are in danger. And if it could happen in Alexandria, if it could happen in Berlin, maybe it could happen somewhere up ahead, and my heroes would be killed." Book burning is a theme that Bradbury used in multiple stories.

Bradbury also wrote in response to the **persecution** that took place during the Red Scare, or fear of **communism**, in the United States. In 1949, Communists had taken over China, and the Communist Soviet Union detonated its first atomic bomb. Fears of communism ran high in the United States during the 1950s.

Established in 1938, the House Un-American Activities Committee (HUAC) investigated charges that both the U.S. government and the Hollywood movie industry were full of communists. Screenwriters, actors, and producers testified in front of a committee led by Senator Joseph McCarthy. They were asked to name names of other possible communists. Some agreed, destroying the careers of those they named, while others refused and were jailed for contempt of Congress. According to Bradbury, "we were very close to panic and wholesale book burning." In reaction to seeing colleagues brought up before the committee, and to widespread fears of atomic weapons, Bradbury wrote the short story that would become *Fahrenheit 451*.

ACTIVITIES

Video

Fahrenheit 451 by Ray Bradbury | Context

Discover some of the real-life events that inspired *Fahrenheit 451* by watching this video.

1. How did the politics of World War II help shape the writing of *Fahrenheit 451*? What parallels can you draw between the real-life burning and censorship of books by the Nazis and dictator Joseph Stalin, and the events of the novel? Cite textual evidence.
2. How did the time period that *Fahrenheit 451* was written in impact Bradbury's creation of the novel? In what ways might the story be different if it were written today?

Document

The Life and Times of Ray Bradbury

Examine the timeline to learn more about Bradbury's life and the historical events of the time.

1. How might magazine subscriptions such as *Amazing Stories* have influenced Bradbury's work? Why were these kinds of stories so important to the young writer?
2. How do you think Bradbury felt about the shift of science fiction magazines from print to digital format? What parallels can you draw between this changing technology and the plot of *Fahrenheit 451*?

RUBRIC

Writing a Short Story

Students will choose an excerpt from the novel and use it as their inspiration in writing a short story. An exemplary short story will meet the following criteria.

- Engages the reader from the opening line
- Establishes a clear, consistent point of view
- Introduces a narrator and a setting
- Develops an engaging conflict at the heart of the narrative to build tension and keep the reader interested
- Develops characters and events through purposeful and well-crafted literary devices
- Creates a logical progression of events in the narrative that build upon each other using various techniques
- Explores ideas, concepts, and writing styles with creativity and originality
- Demonstrates a high level of skill in using appropriate narrative techniques to tell the story
- Concludes the narrative in a thoughtful, effective manner appropriate to the narrative
- Uses varied, purposeful diction and syntax to affect style and serve the narrative
- Writes with clarity, imagination, and a unique, personal voice
- Does not use stereotypes or clichés
- Uses effective, believable dialogue
- Uses correct spelling, grammar, and punctuation

Conflict in the Novel

In literature, conflict is a struggle between two or more opposing forces, creating a tension that must be resolved. This is the main challenge that the protagonist faces throughout the story. This struggle is often between the protagonist and antagonist, but there are other types of conflict as well.

The Four Major Types of Conflict in Literature

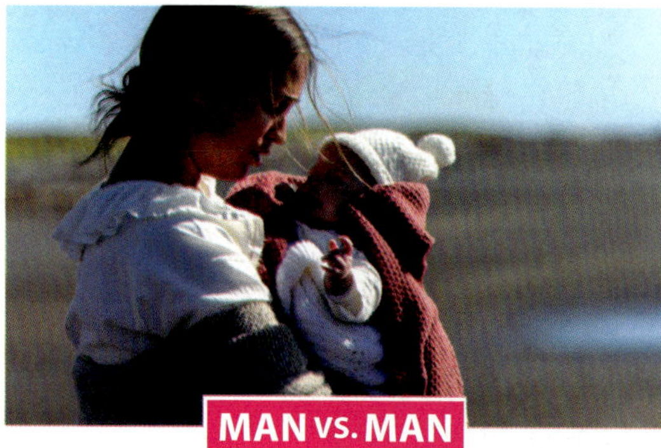

MAN VS. MAN

External conflicts, such as man versus man conflicts, are usually easy to spot. Characters can conflict verbally in arguments or physically in fights. In *The Light between Oceans*, married couple Tom and Isabelle argue about whether or not to pass off a shipwrecked baby as their own child.

MAN VS. SELF

Internal conflicts focus on characters struggling with two opposite emotions or desires and how the characters resolve that struggle. In *Speak*, the protagonist has been assaulted by a fellow high school classmate at a party. Her internal conflict is over whether to tell the police and other students about the attack.

MAN VS. SOCIETY

In a man versus society conflict, an individual does not want to **conform** to the expectations of society or an outside group. The protagonist's morals and values often conflict with those of the larger society, which is an external conflict. In *The Handmaid's Tale*, Offred struggles against the rules of her dystopian society. Even telling her story is a blow against the oppressive culture.

MAN VS. NATURE

Characters who are pit against nature often learn something about themselves or the world in the process. Cheryl Strayed, the author of *Wild*, decides to hike the 1,100-mile (1,770-km) Pacific Crest Trail. She confronts record snow levels, bears, and rattlesnakes along the way. Strayed develops new skills, new insights, and some hard-won peace as a result.

Types of Conflict in *Fahrenheit 451*

There are three main types of conflict in *Fahrenheit 451*. These are man versus self, man versus society, and man versus man. The novel's conflicts drive it forward.

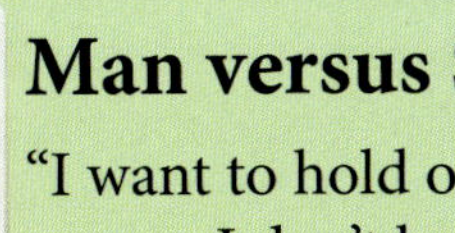

Man versus Self

"I want to hold onto this funny thing. God, it's gotten big on me. I don't know what it is. I'm so damned unhappy. I'm so mad, and I don't know why. I feel like I'm putting on weight. I feel fat. I feel like I've been saving up a lot of things, and don't know what. I might even start reading books."

Montag, Part One

Montag

Beatty

Man versus Society

"'I—I've been thinking. About the fire last week. About the man whose library we fixed. What happened to him?'
'They took him screaming off to the asylum.'
'He wasn't insane.'
Beatty arranged his card quietly. 'Any man's insane who thinks he can fool the government and us.'"

Montag and Beatty, Part One

Man versus Man

"'Let's get back to work,' said Montag, quietly.
Mildred kicked at a book. 'Books aren't people. You read and I look all around, but there isn't anybody!'...
'Now,' said Mildred, 'My 'family' is people. They tell me things: I laugh, they laugh! And the colors!'
'Yes, I know.'
'And besides, if Captain Beatty knew about those books—...He might come and burn the house and the 'family.' That's awful! Think of our investment. Why should I read? What for?'
'What for! Why!' said Montag."

Montag and Mildred, Part Two

ACTIVITIES

 **More**

The Types of Conflict in *Fahrenheit 451*

Analyze the excerpts from the novel revealing the types of conflict as they appear in *Fahrenheit 451*.

1. How do these excerpts of conflict reveal the novel's theme? How do they reveal character? Explain and defend your ideas.
2. Write an analysis of Atwood's development of conflict between Montag and Beatty. What deeper truths may be suggested about these characters as a result of their conflict?

 **Document**

Bradbury's Guy Montag: An Ontology of Conflict and Fire

Review the 2015 article by Kelcy Dolan of Arcadia University.

1. In the article, Dolan observes that there are times in the novel when Montag acts as his own antagonist. What are the results of this? How does this fact affect the reader's ability to relate to Montag?
2. Dolan concludes that, "Montag, more so though than the intellectuals, has the opportunity to help society heal and progress." Do you think this is the case? How well-supported is her argument? Explain your answer with critical analysis.

RUBRIC

Holding a Classroom Debate

Students will form groups and prepare arguments for a debate on a controversial issue. Exemplary performance in a debate will meet the following criteria.

- Demonstrates in-depth understanding of the topic and related information
- Presents strong, logical, and convincing arguments
- Communicates in a clear and confident manner
- Maintains eye contact
- Uses clear vocal tone and a reasonable rate of vocal delivery
- Uses respectful and appropriate language and body language
- Delivers arguments, evidence, and counter-evidence in an engaging and persuasive manner
- Supports each major point of an argument with several relevant and detailed facts and examples
- Connects all arguments to the overall topic in a clear, concise, and organized manner
- Presents the arguments and supporting evidence in a clear, logical manner
- Presents clear, thorough, and accurate information throughout the debate
- Addresses all of the opposing team's arguments with counter-arguments
- Identifies any weakness in the opposing team's arguments
- Constructs strong and relevant counter-arguments using accurate information
- Presents strong and persuasive arguments throughout the debate
- Summarizes the arguments in the closing statement

Introducing the Characters

Characters can include people, animals, or things represented in a literary work. They can entertain, educate, persuade, and teach, depending on what the author wants to accomplish with his or her story. Characters can be based on historical people and events or be completely made up, such as an alien from outer space. A conflict motivates characters to take action.

Major Characters in *Fahrenheit 451*

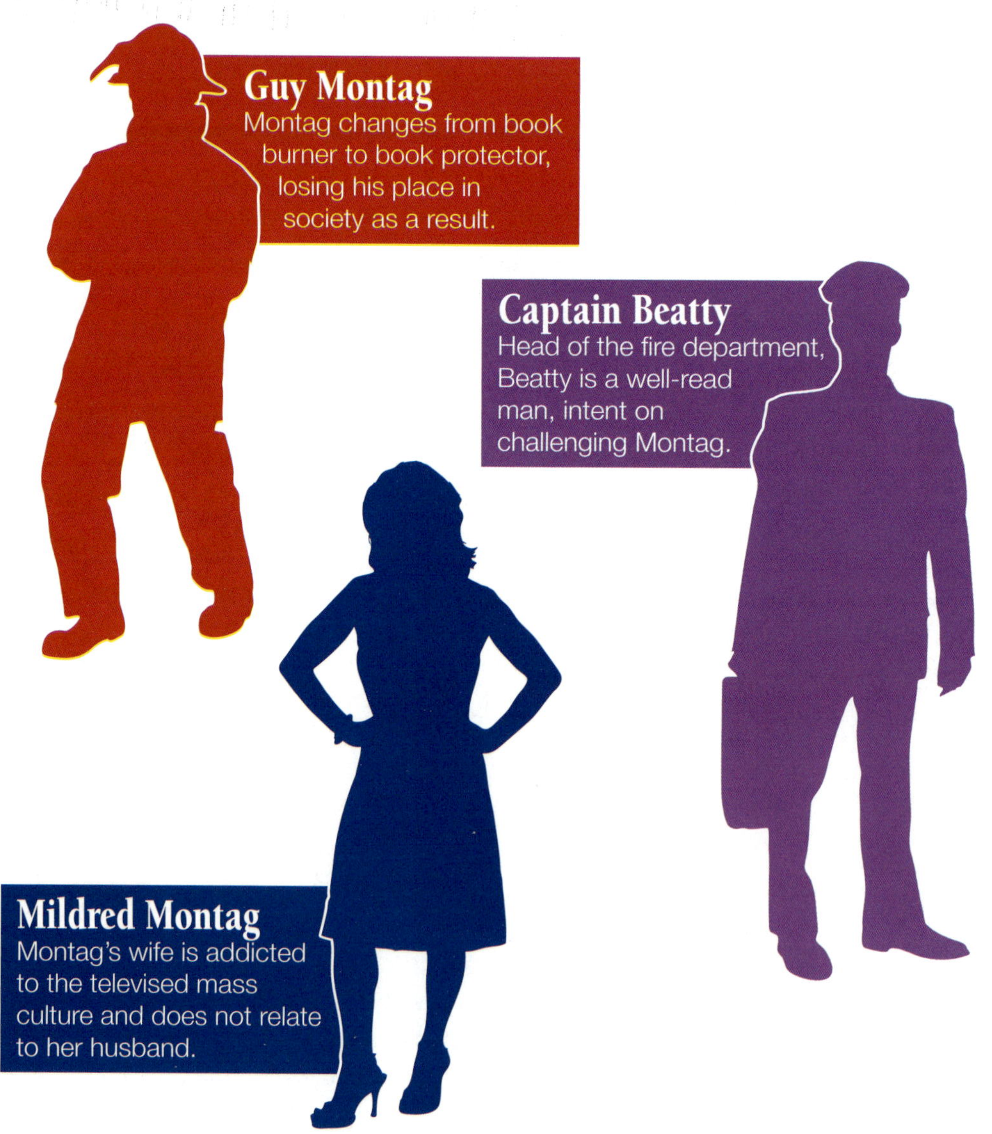

Characters may be protagonists or antagonists. Montag is the protagonist of *Fahrenheit 451*, around whom all action revolves. Both Mildred and Beatty are antagonists who cause conflict for the protagonist.

Characters can be dynamic or static, round or flat, or switch from one to another over the course of a work. A dynamic character changes throughout the story. For example, the dynamic character Montag moves from unthinking fireman to outlaw intellectual. Static characters, such as the fireman Stoneman, do not change over the course of the story. Round characters, such as Beatty, are described in detail, and are realistic and complex, with depth to their character. Since Bradbury does not describe Mrs. Bowles very much, she is a flat character. A foil is a character whose personal qualities stand in contrast to another character's, and frequently, the foil helps bring out the personality of the protagonist. Beatty is a foil for Montag.

Faber
A former university professor, Faber has been hiding both his books and his objections to the larger culture.

The Hound
The Hound is a mechanical tracking and killing machine.

Granger
Montag meets this dissident writer when he runs away from the city.

Clarisse McClellan
A young neighbor, Clarisse's questions encourage Montag's **disaffection** with the larger society.

Stoneman and Black
These two fellow firemen do not question their work.

Mrs. Bowles
A typical example of an everyday citizen, Mrs. Bowles does not reflect on her life.

Mrs. Phelps
This friend of Mildred's shows some feeling when Montag reads a poem.

ACTIVITIES

Weblink

Character Analysis of Guy Montag

Review a character analysis of Montag and debate his role in *Fahrenheit 451*.

1. Montag begins the novel as a fireman who burns books, but by the end, becomes dedicated to memorizing them. Does this transformation justify his past actions? How do the violent acts Montag commits in the novel affect the reader's opinion of him? Give textual evidence to support your claims.
2. Do you consider Montag to be a hero? Why or why not? Support your opinion with specific examples from the text.

More

Character Development in *Fahrenheit 451*

Analyze the characters in *Fahrenheit 451* using the descriptions on the character map and excerpts from each character. Then, choose a character and answer the following questions.

1. Which of the writer's techniques are most effective at revealing this character's traits? Why?
2. In what ways is the characterization of this character ineffective? What could be done to improve this character's function in the novel? Defend your ideas with evidence.

RUBRIC

Creating a Literary Device Analysis Booklet

Students will analyze the author's use of a literary device in the novel, and create a booklet to present this analysis. An exemplary literary device analysis booklet will meet the following criteria.

- Defines the chosen literary device accurately and in detail
- Places the definition of the literary device at the beginning of the booklet
- Provides strong, specific examples of how this literary device is used in the novel
- Describes examples in detail, with quotations properly integrated
- Includes thorough analysis of the use, purpose, and effectiveness of each example of how the chosen literary device is used in the novel
- Arranges all pages logically
- Examples are organized chronologically
- Provides no more than one example and its analysis per page
- Creates a neat, well-organized, and attractive booklet
- Booklet is colorful and displays the student's creativity
- Uses illustrations to represent the chosen literary device and the examples of how it is used in the novel

The Art of Storytelling

Storytelling is a way to entertain, engage with others, teach, or communicate **perspectives** on society. A narrative, or story, is a series of events that is often logically arranged. When writing his or her story, a writer structures the narrative in a particular way. The writer can also use different types of literary devices to create a distinct style and convey the narrative's overall message.

Structure of a Narrative

Each narrative has a structure, which writers keep in mind when creating a story. The most common narrative structure, known as dramatic structure or Freytag's Pyramid, consists of five main components, which are all used in *Fahrenheit 451*.

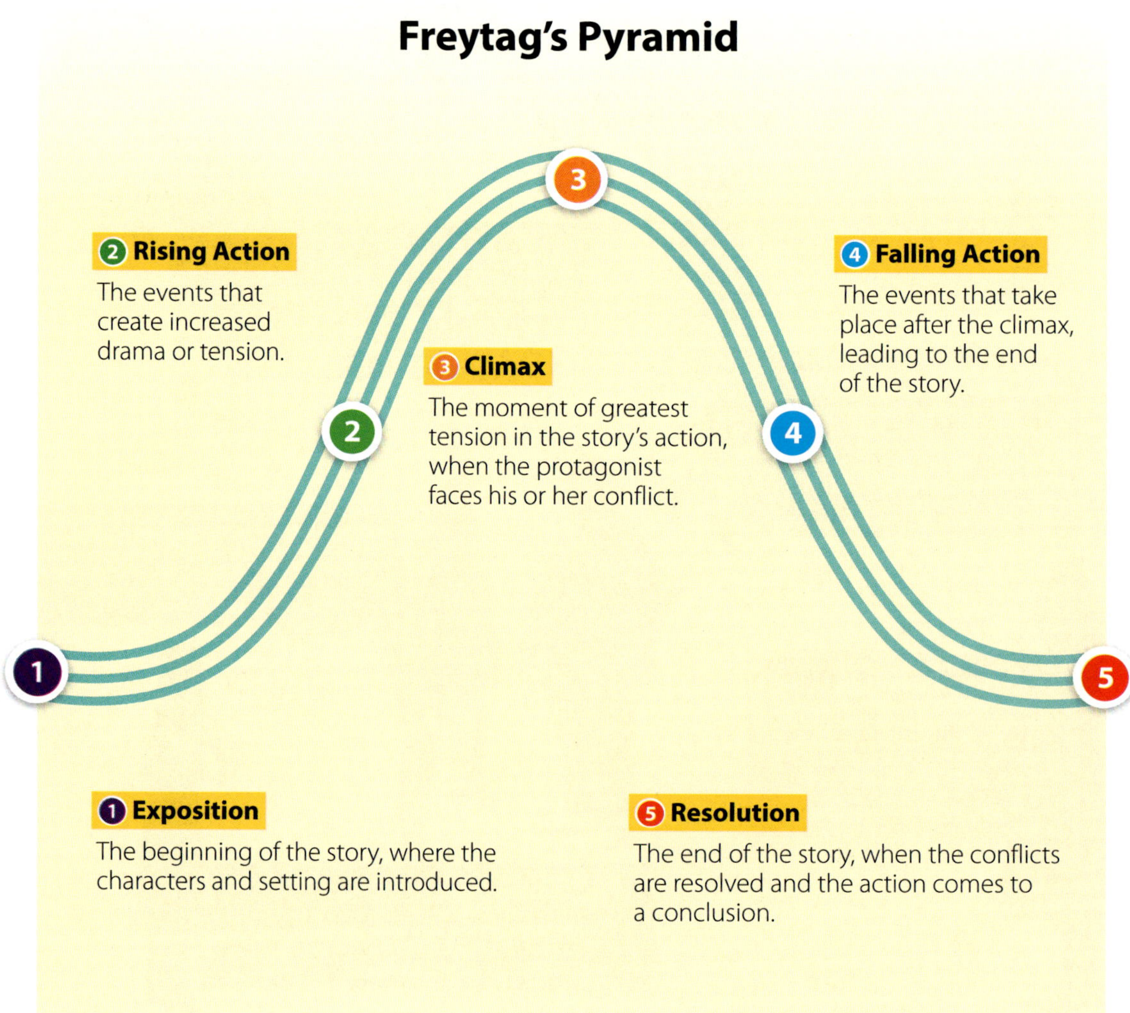

Plot

Every narrative needs a plot, or sequence in which the story's events unfold. The plotline is the order in which events, or plot points, take place. These events build on each other and are organized in a logical manner. Each event causes the next event to happen, thus creating the narrative. Most of *Fahrenheit 451* takes place sequentially, producing an easy-to-follow plot.

Plot Points in Part Three of *Fahrenheit 451*

1. Montag murders Beatty.
2. He goes on the run, trying to avoid the Mechanical Hound.
3. Montag urges Faber to leave the city.
4. He continues to evade the Hound by jumping in the river.
5. He meets the men who have memorized books.
6. The authorities act as if another man is Montag and kill him.
7. Bombs destroy the city.
8. Montag and the other men head back to the city.

Literary Devices

Literary devices are specific tools that add meaning or create more compelling stories. Writers use these devices to add depth, insight, and suspense to their stories. The two types of literary devices are literary elements and literary techniques.

ACTIVITIES

Weblink

Rhetorical Question
Learn more about rhetorical questions and their use in literature by reading this article.

1. What purposes do Beatty's rhetorical questions serve? Give specific examples from the novel.
2. Are rhetorical questions in literature as important as they are in daily language? Why do you think so? Give evidence to support your opinion.

More

Examples of Literary Techniques from the Novel
Analyze the author's use of literary techniques and how they contribute to the narrative of *Fahrenheit 451*.

1. Choose one literary technique used in the novel. In what particular way did the author use this literary technique? How effective was its usage?
2. What arguments can be made for the use of your chosen literary technique in a text? If this technique were overused or underutilized, what effect might it have on an author's work?

Theme in the Novel

Often open to interpretation, the themes of a story are the ideas or positions underlying the topic. Themes are frequently general, universal statements about life that can be expressed through the events that take place in the story, the ideas repeated along the way, and the lessons that the characters learn. A reader may have to examine many different aspects of the novel to form an opinion about the themes. Major themes appear throughout the narrative, while the author may reveal minor themes only a few times. The topic of a narrative is different than its theme. The topic is the narrative's subject matter, or what it is written about, while a theme makes a statement about the topic itself.

Values

Closely related to the novel's themes are the values held by the novel's characters. The way in which characters act, react, and respond to their world helps reveal the theme and values of the character, author, and story. In any novel, different characters uphold different values. Sometimes, these values will inform or become the basis of a particular theme in the novel.

Major Themes of *Fahrenheit 451*

Bradbury's major themes reflect the worries of his time. He was concerned by the censorship of books about political thought. Technology, in the form of the atom bomb and the television set, changed the way people viewed their world in the 1950s, and it seemed to Bradbury as if the world could end at any minute.

Censorship

"If you don't want a man unhappy politically, don't give him two sides to a question to worry him; give him one. Better yet, give him none. Let him forget there is such a thing as war. If the government is inefficient, top-heavy, and tax-mad, better it be all those than that people worry over it. Peace, Montag. Give the people contests they win by remembering the words to more popular songs or the names of state capitals or how much corn Iowa grew last year. Cram them full of noncombustible data, chock them so damned full of 'facts' they feel stuffed, but absolutely 'brilliant' with information. Then they'll feel they're thinking, they'll get a sense of motion without moving. And they'll be happy, because facts of that sort don't change."

Beatty, Part One

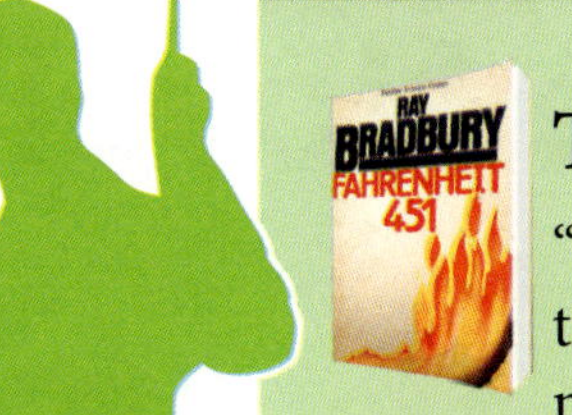

Trouble with Technology

"But who has ever torn himself from the claw that encloses you when you drop a seed in a TV parlour? It grows you any shape it wishes! It is an environment as real as the world. It becomes and is the truth. Books can be beaten down with reason. But with all my knowledge and scepticism, I have never been able to argue with a one-hundred-piece symphony orchestra, full colour, three dimensions, and I being in and part of those incredible parlours."

Faber, Part Two

Faber

Beatty

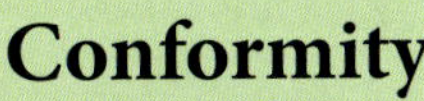

Conformity

"Surely you remember the boy in your own school class who was exceptionally 'bright,' did most of the reciting and answering while the others sat like so many leaden idols, hating him. And wasn't it this bright boy you selected for beatings and tortures after hours? Of course it was. We must all be alike. Not everyone born free and equal, as the Constitution says, but everyone made equal. Each man the image of every other; then all are happy, for there are no mountains to make them cower, to judge themselves against."

Beatty, Part One

Secondary Themes

Secondary or minor themes are motifs that are not strongly emphasized in the narrative. They work with a novel's major themes to help the reader gain an understanding of the story and the characters. Secondary themes in *Fahrenheit 451* include the allure of the past, the value of imagination, and the transformation of one thing into another.

ACTIVITIES

Video

Fahrenheit 451 by Ray Bradbury | Themes

Learn more about theme in *Fahrenheit 451* by watching this video.

1. How do books transform Montag from a conformist to a rebel, and then to a leader? Why does reading give him means for both personal and social change? What are the effects of these changes?
2. In what ways do books connect people to each other? How do the themes Bradbury uses help readers to connect with Montag's story? Give specific examples from the novel.

More

Major and Secondary Themes

Analyze the author's development of themes over the course of the novel.

1. Choose a secondary theme from this spread and analyze its appearances in the novel. How does this theme first emerge? Which is the most poignant example of this theme in the novel?
2. What particular commentary might the author be making about life as a result of this theme's presence in the text? Explain and defend your ideas.
3. Choose a major theme presented on pages 16–17. In what ways does your chosen secondary theme relate to this major theme? Does it deepen or detract from the major theme? How or in what way?

RUBRIC

Creating a Symbolism Poster

Students will choose one of the other symbols listed on page 19 and analyze its role in the novel. They will then create a poster to present their analysis. An exemplary symbolism poster will meet the following criteria.

- Presents a clear purpose that is conveyed throughout the poster
- Shows an understanding of the concept of symbolism and the role it has in the novel
- Provides an in-depth analysis of what the symbol represents
- Discusses the role the symbol has in the novel
- Clearly indicates where the symbol appears in the novel
- Uses specific, detailed examples from the text to support the analysis
- Makes clear connections to the text
- Properly integrates all quotations
- Organizes the information in a logical, easy-to-read manner
- Includes high-quality graphics that relate to the symbol and effectively enhance understanding of the topic
- Features clear and concise writing
- Uses correct spelling, grammar, and punctuation
- Clearly labels items of importance
- Headings and subheadings are clear and easy to read
- Uses layout to creatively enhances the information
- Creates a poster that is attractive in terms of layout, design, and organization
- Shows a strong effort by the student

Symbolism in the Novel

A symbol is a person, place, action, or thing that stands for something beyond itself. **Tangible** concepts, symbols represent intangible things. An author uses symbolism to create a specific mood or emotion in a story. Symbols help create coherence within the narrative. If they are repeated throughout a story, symbols often gain meaning and strength, and their meaning can change throughout the book. When studying a work of literature, the reader can gain a deeper understanding of the story by identifying and analyzing its symbols.

Beatty

What Is Fire?

"'What is there about fire that's so lovely? No matter what age we are, what draws us to it?' Beatty blew out the flame and lit it again. 'It's perpetual motion; the thing man wanted to invent but never did. Or almost perpetual motion. If you let it go on, it'd burn our lifetimes out. What is fire? It's a mystery. Scientists give us gobbledegook about friction and molecules. But they don't really know. Its real beauty is that it destroys responsibility and consequences. A problem gets too burdensome, then into the furnace with it."

Beatty, Part Three

Fire as a Symbol

In *Fahrenheit 451*, fire stands as a symbol of both destruction and creative potential. In addition, it acts as an emblem of technology. Written after the first atomic bombs were dropped in Japan, the book features the central image of fire devastating homes, and finally, whole cities. Thus, it had a particular impact for readers when it was published. By the end of the novel, Montag moves from the raging fire of his own house to the comforting blaze of Granger's campfire. The men around it, who contain specific books in their memories, wait to recreate the literature when society is ready. Fire becomes a symbol of home and hearth.

Who Connects with Fire?

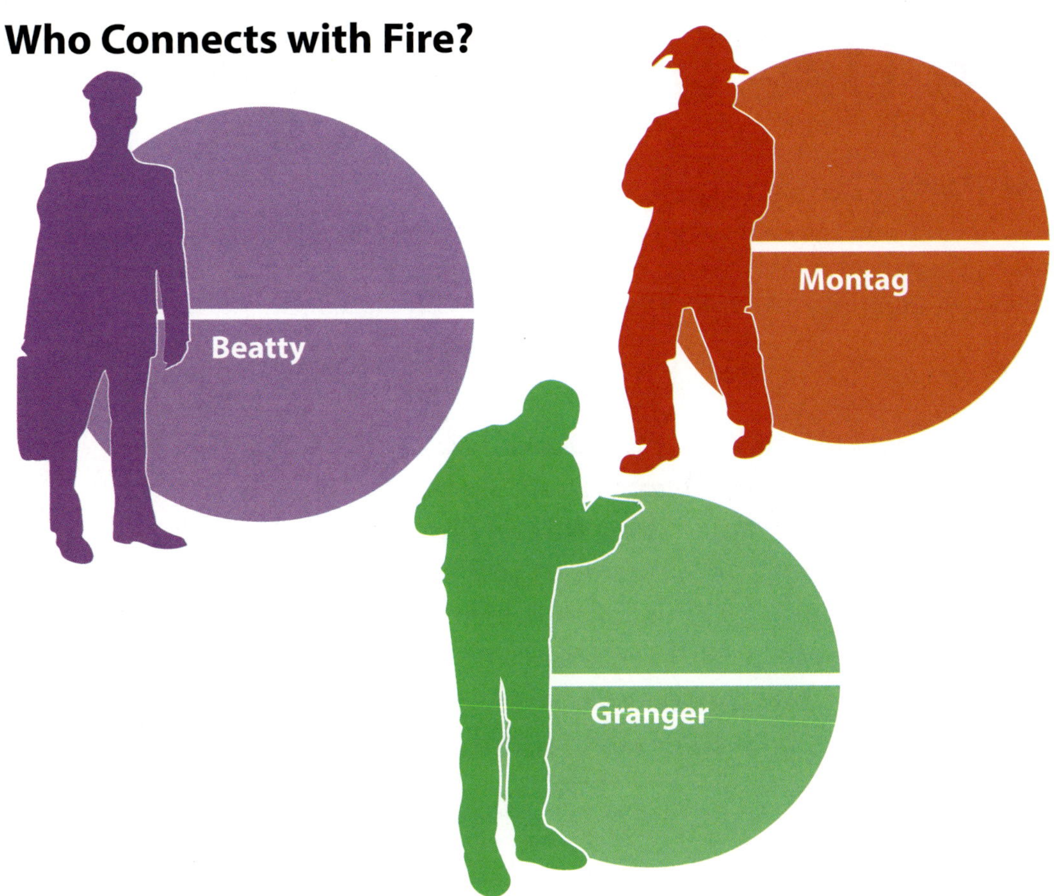

Other Symbols in the Novel

The Phoenix

In ancient Egyptian mythology, the phoenix is a bird that burns itself to death at least every 500 years and arises from the ashes as a young bird. Beatty wears a phoenix crest and rides in a Phoenix car. He burns to death, which symbolically illustrates his rebirth.

Mrs. Bowles and Mrs. Phelps

Bradbury uses many variations on the image of fire to describe these friends of Mildred. With their "Cheshire Cat smiles burning through the walls of the house" and "sun-fired hair," they look at their "blazing fingernails." The women are consumed by the violence and mindless distractions of their society. They represent people burning themselves out from the inside.

Salamanders

In ancient mythologies, salamanders could endure living in fires, becoming a symbol of survival. In *Fahrenheit 451*, salamander images appear on the firemen's uniforms. The firemen also call their fire truck a salamander, and Montag himself is like a salamander, since he lives in a fiery environment and escapes from it.

ACTIVITIES

More

What Symbols Appear in the Novel?
Assess the author's use of symbolism in the novel.

1. Choose an example from the chart and analyze what the symbol of fire represents for that character. For which character is this symbol the most poignant in the novel? For which character is the symbol least poignant? Argue your opinions with clear reasons.
2. How is this symbol used or reflected in the novel's themes? Illustrate the ways in which the author's use of language deepens or weakens the meaning of the symbol. Explain and defend your ideas.

Weblink

The Complete Guide to Symbolism
Examine the blog post discussing the usage of symbolism in literature.

1. Contrast and compare examples of analytical descriptions of feelings and sensory descriptions using symbolism from the novel. Which kind is more effective in the novel? Provide reasons for your ideas.
2. Should analytical descriptions play a considerable role in the language of a novel? Why or why not?

RUBRIC

Analyzing a Video

Students will watch and assess a video related to a component of the novel, and write an analysis of the video. An exemplary video analysis will meet the following criteria.

- Identifies the purpose of the video
- Identifies the intended audience of the video
- Describes how the content of the video is presented
- Summarizes the information and opinions presented in the video
- Analyzes the quality of the content presented in the video
- Assesses the effectiveness of the video
- Discusses the technical aspects of the video and whether or not these enhance the content
- Determines whether the images and graphics used in the video relate to the content
- Determines whether the video is easy to follow and understand
- Gives the analysis a clear and consistent purpose
- Organizes the analysis in a logical, effective manner
- Presents a strong, clear argument about the video
- Provides strong and accurate details to support the argument about the video
- Considers other perspectives on the purpose and effectiveness of the video
- Makes connections between the video and the novel
- Properly integrates quotations from the video
- Cites all sources used in the analysis

The Use of Language

Fast-Paced Language

With words tumbling over each other and repeated, Bradbury's writing gives a sense of speed and urgency. That speed gives the reader the feeling that a character cannot communicate his or her thoughts quickly enough. It also adds drama.

"Speed up the film, Montag, quick. Click, Pic, Look, Eye, Now, Flick, Here, There, Swift, Pace, Up, Down, In, Out, Why, How, Who, What, Where, Eh? Uh! Bang! Smack! Wallop, Bing, Bong, Boom! Digest-digests, digest-digest-digests. Politics? One column, two sentences a headline! Then, in midair, all vanishes! Whirl man's mind around about so fast under the pumping hands of publishers, exploiters, broadcasters that the centrifuge flings off all unnecessary, time-wasting thought!"

Opposite Meanings

Bradbury subverts language. Instead of a spouse and possibly children, a "family" consists of the characters on TV, and firemen destroy houses instead of saving them. The Hound is not man's best friend, but a hunting and killing machine, and a seashell does not echo the sound of the sea, but instead plays unending words and music.

"The Hound leapt up into the air with a rhythm and a sense of timing that was incredibly beautiful. Its needle shot out. It was suspended for a moment in their gaze, as if to give the vast audience time to appreciate everything, the raw look of the victim's face, the empty street, the steel animal a bullet nosing the target."

Use of Punctuation

Bradbury uses a variety of punctuation within a paragraph. His choices have different effects. They can slow down or speed up the rhythm of the language.

"A great thunderstorm of sound gushed from the walls. Music bombarded him at such an immense volume that his bones were almost shaken from their tendons; he felt his jaw vibrate, his eyes wobble in his head. He was a victim of concussion. When it was all over he felt like a man who had been thrown from a cliff, whirled in a centrifuge, and spat out over a waterfall that fell and fell into emptiness and emptiness and never—quite—touched—bottom—never—never—quite—no not quite—touched bottom...and you fell so fast you didn't touch the sides either...never...quite... touched ...anything."

Descriptive Language

Bradbury's writing is not a clinical dissection of a society gone wrong. Instead, his language is highly charged and imaginative. Long strings of description fill entire paragraphs.

"The train radio vomited upon Montag, in retaliation, a great tonload of music made of tin, copper, silver, chromium, and brass. The people were pounded into submission; they did not run, there was no place to run; the great air train fell down its shaft in the earth."

Use of Contradiction

Bradbury uses antonyms and opposition throughout the novel. While Montag's work life is filled with fire and burning, his home life is cold and dark. Clarisse is described as a candle in the dark, warm and nurturing, while Mildred is cold and distant.

"'What for! Why!' said Montag. 'I saw the...snake in the world the other night. It was dead but it was alive. It could see but it couldn't see.'"

ACTIVITIES

Video

Feeling More Alive: Fahrenheit 451's The Hearth and the Salamander

Explore author John Green's views on *Fahrenheit 451* by watching this video.

1. In the video, John makes the observation that "everything is both alive and dead in *Fahrenheit 451*." What does he mean by this? How does this contradiction affect the way the characters are perceived by the reader?
2. John quotes Beatty in the video, when he says, "we made the world in which we live, not some all powerful other." Why is this a necessary distinction to make? How does this statement shape the reader's understanding of the events of the novel? What was Bradbury attempting to warn readers about by including this line in the book?

Document

The Life of the Mind and a Life of Meaning: Reflections on *Fahrenheit 451*

Review the 2009 article by Rodney A. Smolla of the Washington and Lee University School of Law.

1. Who do you think is the intended audience for this document? Why? Are the tone and language used appropriate for this audience? Explain your answer.
2. What are the main points of the document and how are they presented? Are these points conveyed effectively to the reader? Why or why not?

Impact of the Novel at the Time of Publishing

Reception of the novel has been mixed. Many reviewers liked Bradbury's emphasis on the dangers of censorship and admired his attack on mass culture in the form of television, while other critics objected to Bradbury setting up intellectuals, in the form of the wandering "dust jackets," in opposition to the mass of ordinary people. They found him elitist, that is, someone who thinks that a society should be dominated by a small group of powerful scholarly people. Critics also accused him of having no faith in the masses' ability to govern or think critically.

Too Obscure?

Some reviewers focused on Bradbury's more obscure references, such as Plato's *Allegory of the Cave* or *Gulliver's Travels*. When the old woman burns along with her books, she says, "Play the man, Master Ridley; we shall this day light such a candle, by God's grace, in England, as I trust shall never be put out." This quote refers to two men being burnt alive for their religious beliefs in England in 1555, an event which few people would recognize.

Television as a Bad Guy

Critics have objected to Bradbury's assertion that television is responsible for turning people into mindless consumers. By turning from literature to television, Bradbury's society has instigated the burning of books. The critics contend that television is just another way of gaining information.

Banned Book

Fahrenheit 451 has been controversial since its publication and has often appeared on the American Library Association's top 100 banned books list. Some parents and school administrators objected to the book being required reading for middle school and high school students. They pointed to the use of profanity and questionable themes.

The Author Objects

In the late 1960s, Bradbury's publisher put together a new version of *Fahrenheit 451* in which the editors changed about 75 separate sections. According to Bradbury, they were "fearful of contaminating the young." During the 1970s, the only copy of *Fahrenheit 451* that readers could buy was the censored one. Students figured out that they were not reading the original text and wrote to the author to complain, which Bradbury called "an exquisite irony," since the book deals with censorship in the future. He blasted the revisions and insisted that the book be reprinted with every word in its original place.

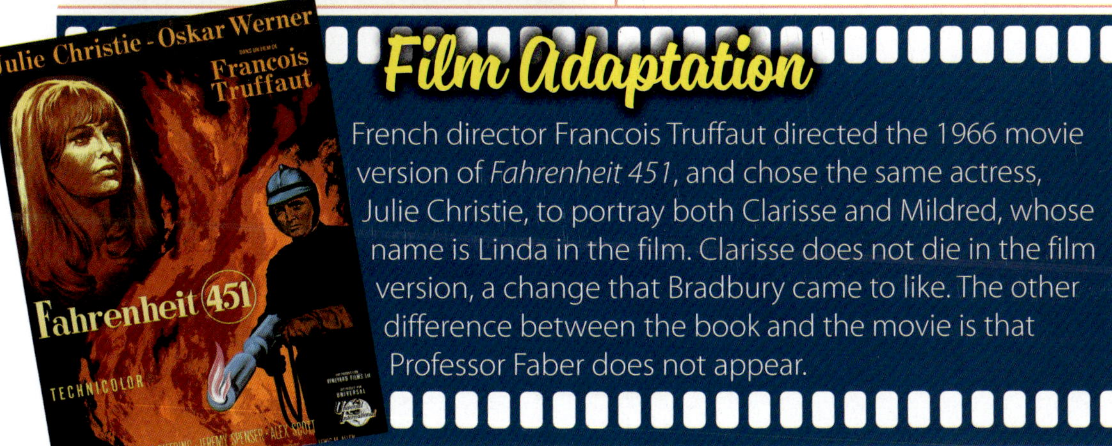

Film Adaptation

French director Francois Truffaut directed the 1966 movie version of *Fahrenheit 451*, and chose the same actress, Julie Christie, to portray both Clarisse and Mildred, whose name is Linda in the film. Clarisse does not die in the film version, a change that Bradbury came to like. The other difference between the book and the movie is that Professor Faber does not appear.

ACTIVITIES

Video

FAHRENHEIT 451. Interview with Ray Bradbury.

Discover more about Bradbury's creation of *Fahrenheit 451* by watching this video interviewer with the author.

1. In the interview, Bradbury recounts how he chose the names Montag and Faber, and did not realize why until years later. Why are these character names appropriate? How much of a novel is the result of deliberate choices by the author, versus subconscious decisions, such as the ones Bradbury describes? Why do you think this is the case?
2. Bradbury explains that the threat of atomic war was fresh in his mind when he wrote *Fahrenheit 451*. How did this threat affect the development of the novel? Do you agree with Bradbury's assertion that the real threat is ignorance and lack of education? How is this exemplified in the novel?

Weblink

Back in '53

Find out more about the novel's initial critical reception in this blog post by Phil Nichols.

1. Nichols discusses one of the first reviews of Fahrenheit 451, by editor J. Francis McComas, who accused Bradbury of appealing "exclusively to the emotions." Is this a fair assessment? Why or why not?
2. McComas is critical of the lack of detail regarding the atomic war in the novel, but Nichols attributes this to the fact that the story is told from Montag's limited perspective. Which perspective do you agree with the most? Give reasons to support your answer.

RUBRIC

Analyzing Bias in a Document

Students will analyze the bias that exists in a document, and how that bias shapes the opinions presented in the document. An exemplary analysis of bias in a document will meet the following criteria.

- Identifies the main points presented in the document
- Offers an in-depth interpretation of the document
- Differentiates between facts and opinions
- Identifies the writer
- Presents information about the writer
- Assesses the writer's reliability
- Determines the goals for the document
- Considers and assesses the writer's perspective
- Determines the writer's intended audience
- Identifies when and where the document was written
- Describes the historical context for the time and place in which the document was created, and analyzes how this context might have shaped the opinions expressed in the document
- Infers political or societal influences that may have shaped the opinions presented in the document
- Determines whether the writer had first-hand knowledge of the topic or event, or whether they are reporting as a secondary source
- Determines the document's bias
- Infers what interests the writer might have had that led them to create this document
- Explores other sources related to the topic of the document

Impact of the Novel Now

With the recent rise in popularity of dystopian fiction, renewed attention is being paid to *Fahrenheit 451*. A new adaptation of the book will appear on HBO in 2018. It is clear that Bradbury's novel predicted the media's impact on people's lives, as issues regarding fears of media control of information are still being debated today.

Contradicting Himself

In 2007, Bradbury claimed in an interview that *Fahrenheit 451* was not a reaction to the McCarthy era of hunting for communists. He has also said that he was not commenting on government censorship, and insisted that the novel was primarily about how television can destroy people's interest in reading books. However, close friend, frequent interviewer, and biographer Sam Weller disagrees. Weller argued that while the novel does warn about television and its pitfalls, it also reflects Bradbury's distrust of censorship, book burning, and communist hunting.

In **2011**, Bradbury finally allowed *Fahrenheit 451* to be released as an **e-book**, after calling the internet **"meaningless"** and **"a big distraction."**

Since its **publication**, *Fahrenheit 451* has sold **more than 10 million** copies.

Fahrenheit 451 was made into a video game in **1984**.

ACTIVITIES

A Rewarding Life

Bradbury has received a number of awards for his work. He became a movie legend when he received a star on the Hollywood Walk of Fame in 2002. In 2004, President George W. Bush bestowed on him the National Medal of Arts, the highest award given by the U.S. government to artists and art patrons. Three years later, he received a special Pulitzer Prize citation "for his distinguished, prolific, and deeply influential career as an unmatched author of science fiction and fantasy." Bradbury was conscious of the richness of his life, noting in 1983, "I can't name a writer who's had a more perfect life. My books are all in print, I'm in all the school libraries, and when I go places I get the applause at the start of my speech." After his death in 2012, President Barack Obama said of Bradbury, "His gift for storytelling reshaped our culture and expanded our world."

In 2009, artist Tim Hamilton produced an authorized graphic version of *Fahrenheit 451*. A comic collector since the age of nine, Bradbury wrote the introduction. The book looks like a classic comic.

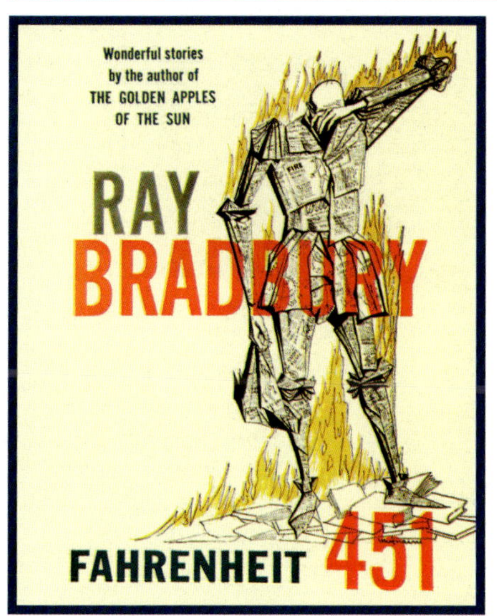

A Change in Format

Book designers have been intrigued with the look of *Fahrenheit 451* since its publication and have become creative with their packaging. In 1953, 200 copies of the book were bound in asbestos, a fire-resistant material. In 2017, French designers put out an edition of the book that appeared to be entirely in black until a flame held close to the book revealed the printed words.

First Hand

Ramin Bahrani on the Challenge of Updating 'Fahrenheit 451' for Modern Audiences

Examine this interview with Ramin Bahrani, director of the 2018 HBO adaptation of *Fahrenheit 451*.

1. Bahrani points out that if physical books were burned today, they could just be downloaded again. Given the widespread popularity of e-readers and other methods of digital consumption, how is it possible to adapt Bradbury's story to today's world? What changes must be made to ensure there are no plot holes? If you were the filmmaker, how would you address these and other challenges of adapting *Fahrenheit 451* for a modern audience?
2. Bahrani talks about how Bradbury adapted the novel as a musical and a play, and some of the changes he made and approved. How would the novel be different if Clarisse had survived? What effect would this have had on Montag? Explain your answer.

Document

Ray Bradbury Reveals the True Meaning of *Fahrenheit 451*

Find out more about Bradbury's claims by reading this article.

1. Bradbury is quoted as saying that the novel is not, in fact, about government censorship or a response to McCarthyism. Do you believe his claim? Why or why not? Are writers inherently biased when it comes to analyzing their own writing? Give reasons for your answer.
2. Do writers have a say in the way their work is interpreted or is it up to readers to decide for themselves? Why do you think so?

RUBRIC

Creating a Timeline

Students will explore a topic related to the novel and create a timeline to present their research on historical events connected to this topic. An exemplary timeline will meet the following criteria.

- Includes the most significant events pertaining to the topic to be compared and analyzed
- Includes interesting events
- Uses accurate information for all events, including date, location, and major details
- Orders the events in a chronological sequence
- Describes each event with accurate, vivid, and specific details
- Presents the topic from three or more perspectives
- Inspires the reader to ask thoughtful questions regarding the events and perspectives presented in the timeline
- Uses correct spelling, grammar, and punctuation
- Presents the timeline in a visually attractive and striking manner
- Presents the timeline in a neat, organized manner that is logical and easy to follow
- Uses creativity to present the timeline in an engaging manner
- Effectively communicates the historical information relating to the topic
- Supports each event with reliable sources
- Expresses a clear purpose for creating the timeline
- Enhances the reader's understanding of the topic
- Includes a correctly formatted bibliography of all sources used to create the timeline

Perspectives on Information Suppression

Book burning and other forms of suppressing information have been going on for centuries. In 213 BC, Chinese emperor Qin Shi Huang ordered thousands of books to be thrown upon bonfires. He targeted books of history, philosophy, and poetry so that his regime could not be compared to previous ones and as a way of consolidating power. Since then, other rulers and governments have taken similar actions to suppress information.

Timeline of Governmental Information Suppression

1920s 1930s 1940s 1950s 1960s

1929 Joseph Stalin becomes the dictator of the Union of Soviet Socialist Republics (USSR), and under his rule, the Soviets ban questionable books and kill or imprison their authors.

1948 Under leader Kim Il-Sung, and later his son and grandson, North Korea controls all publications within the country.

1948 Residents of Binghamton, New York, and other communities go door to door in search of comic books to burn, fearing that they encourage moral wickedness.

1956 The U.S. government orders the burning of 6 tons (5.4 tonnes) of books by Wilhelm Reich, including *Character Analysis* and *The Mass Psychology of Fascism*. In 1936, Reich had fled Germany because of book burning.

1966 Chinese leader Mao Zedong starts the Cultural Revolution by shutting down schools and burning books. He encourages urban youth groups called the Red Guard to attack, torture, and often kill intellectuals, artists, and the elderly.

Sometimes information suppression takes the form of burning, and other times it takes the form of banning books and films. Suppression can lead to the destruction of religious structures as a way of destroying historical information. It can also mean controlling various media, by shutting down newspapers, blocking websites, or slowing internet traffic.

1971 Military analyst Daniel Ellsberg leaks parts of a classified 7,000-page government report that undercuts the U.S. rationale for the Vietnam War. *The New York Times* publishes these Pentagon Papers, and the U.S. government takes the Ellsberg case to the Supreme Court.

2013 U.S. intelligence contractor Edward Snowden releases National Security Agency documents revealing secret surveillance programs that gathered the telephone records of tens of millions of Americans. The government charges him with being a spy.

1970s 1980s 1990s 2000s

1996 The Taliban, a violent Islamist political faction, takes control of Afghanistan, burning books, destroying non-Muslim religious works, and prohibiting females from attending school.

2017 Many references to climate change, energy, science, and the environment are removed from U.S. governmental websites.

1993 The World Wide Web is made available to the public. Once it reaches China, the Chinese government seeks to monitor and control how it is used by citizens. Today, the Chinese government continues to restrict access and block websites that it cannot control.

ACTIVITIES

Transparency–Timeline

Timeline of Governmental Information Suppression

Examine the historical and cultural contexts shown on the timeline. Then, contrast and correlate its elements with the themes and events presented in *Fahrenheit 451*.

1. In what ways can historical events, culture, and social mores influence a population's perspective on information suppression? How might these elements have shaped the way a reader in the 1950s interpreted the novel?
2. How might the era in which Ray Bradbury wrote *Fahrenheit 451* have influenced the novel's themes and settings? Where in the novel is this most evident? Explain your reasoning.
3. Which current events, changes in laws, new ideas, or political discussions are shaping the spread of information in the United States today? Which ideas and attitudes are still prevailing? Why?
4. How might current events and present perspectives affect the way a reader interprets the novel? Why is it important for readers to understand the era and context in which a novel is written?

RUBRIC

Writing a Comparative Essay

Students will compare two literary devices used in the novel, and then write a comparative essay based on their analysis. An exemplary comparative essay will meet the following criteria.

- Consists of a one-paragraph introduction, three body paragraphs, and a one-paragraph conclusion
- Introduction includes an engaging lead statement about the topic of the essay, more detailed information about the novel, and a one-sentence thesis that specifically states the essay's argument
- Body paragraphs include a topic sentence that refers to the thesis and how the idea appears in the novel, a supporting sentence that points to this part of the novel, textual evidence of this idea from the novel, and analysis of this evidence
- Body paragraphs end with a transition to the next paragraph
- Conclusion refers to the topic of the essay and the three points presented in the body paragraphs, and restates the thesis
- Provides a thorough analysis of the literary devices in question
- Cites strong and thorough textual evidence to support analysis of what the novel says explicitly
- Presents a clear, specific thesis that indicates a high level of critical engagement
- Organizes ideas in a logical manner
- Communicates arguments in a clear, effective manner
- Properly integrates all quotations
- Correctly cites all sources used
- Correctly formats bibliography

Writing a Comparative Essay

Fahrenheit 451 features several major characters who are described in urgent, symbolic language. Choose two characters from the novel and make a list of their attributes. Compare and contrast the attributes of the two characters, and decide how they are similar and how they are different. Then, write an essay arguing your conclusion, being sure to support your argument with logical reasoning and evidence from the novel.

How to Analyze and Compare Characters

Use the chart to guide your comparison of two characters in *Fahrenheit 451*.

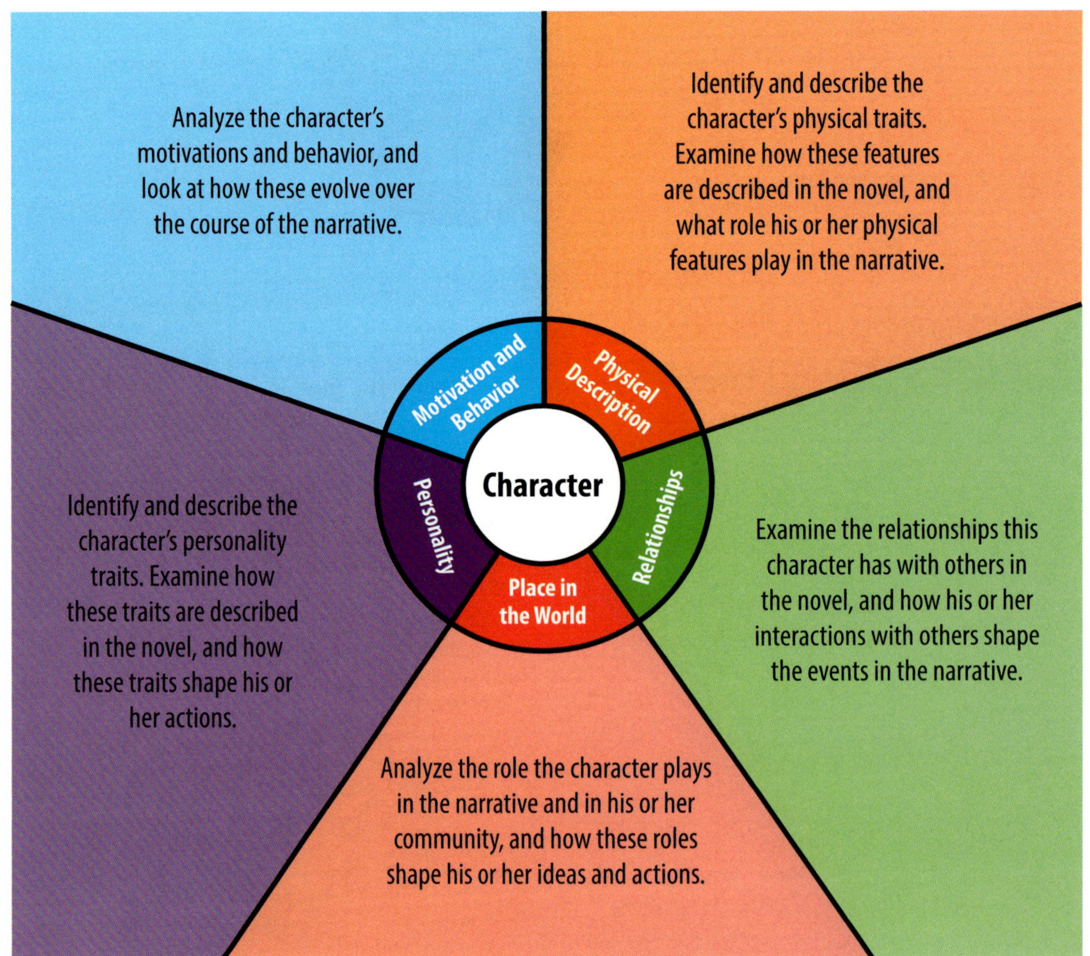

Comparing Montag and Beatty

Montag

Place in the World
- Protagonist of the novel
- Originally a burner of books
- Ultimately rebels against society

Motivation and Behavior
- At first, is energized by burning books
- Feels like his hands act on their own, without connection to his will
- Feels guilt for hiding books
- Tries to reclaim his own humanity
- Frustrated and confused
- Dealing with personal crises throughout novel

Personality
- Intelligent
- Rash and easily swayed
- Observant
- Free-thinking

Relationships
- Married to Mildred
- Once loved his wife, but now feels disconnected from her
- Stands apart from other firemen
- Likes Clarisse and her questions about his life and work
- Is unnerved by Captain Beatty

Physical Description
- Black hair
- 30 years old
- Black brows
- Fiery face
- Has the beginnings of a beard

Beatty

Place in the World
- Powerful man
- Head of the fire department
- One of the antagonists in the novel
- Enforcer of censorship of books

Motivation and Behavior
- Was passionate about books at some point
- Wants to live an unthinking life now
- Manipulates Montag with quotes and arguments
- Wants to die
- Taunts Montag until he burns the captain to death

Relationships
- Dismissive of Mildred
- Tries to control Montag
- Friends with other firemen

Physical Description
- Pipe smoker
- Ruddy face

Personality
- Intelligent
- Well-read
- Likes to argue
- Plays games around power
- Shrewd
- Ruthless
- Condescending
- Inquisitive

ACTIVITIES

More

Questions for Character Analysis

Analyze how specific character features, such as conflicts, motivations, relationships, place in the world, and personality affect the plot of *Fahrenheit 451*. Cite strong and thorough textual evidence to support your analysis of what the novel says explicitly as well as the inferences you may have drawn from the novel's setting, themes, and symbols.

Quiz Answers

1. C
2. C
3. A
4. D
5. B
6. D
7. C
8. C
9. B
10. A

Key Words

communism: a system of government in which a single party controls all businesses and agriculture. Under communism, all property is supposed to be publicly owned, and people work and are paid according to their abilities

conform: to comply or behave according to a group's expectations

disaffection: a lack of connection

dystopia: an imaginary state where everything is unpleasant

fanzine: a magazine produced by amateurs for fans of a particular kind of entertainment

Nazis: German fascist party led by Adolf Hitler. The Nazis were strongly against Jewish people, and thought they were responsible for the widespread poverty during the Great Depression, and for destroying German culture

persecution: cruel or unfair treatment for a long time because of one's religion, race, or political beliefs

perspectives: particular attitudes or points of view

sedate: to make someone feel calm or put them to sleep

tangible: something that can be assessed through the senses

technology: methods of using scientific discoveries for practical purposes

Literary Terms

action: everything that occurs in a narrative

antagonist: the character who stands in opposition to the protagonist; in some cases, the antagonist creates or represents the conflict that the protagonist faces

characterization: the act of describing a character through the person's appearance and personality

climax: the moment of greatest tension in the story's action

conflict: a struggle between two or more opposing forces, creating a tension that must be resolved

exposition: the beginning of the story, where the characters and setting are introduced

falling action: the events that take place after the climax, leading up to the end of the story

Freytag's Pyramid: a narrative structure consisting of five elements; this includes exposition, rising action, climax, falling action, and resolution

metaphor: a symbol used in a story as a literary technique

narrative: a logically arranged series of events presented for an audience; a story

plot: the events that take place in a story

protagonist: the person or thing that acts in opposition to the antagonist

resolution: the end of the story, when the problems are resolved and the action comes to a conclusion

rising action: the events that create increased drama or tension

simile: a comparison between two things using the word "like" or "as"

symbolism: a stylistic device using symbols to represent and intensify concepts and ideas

theme: the underlying topic of main idea of a story

Index

LIGHTBOX

SUPPLEMENTARY RESOURCES

Click on the plus icon ⊕ found in the bottom left corner of each spread to open additional teacher resources.

- Download and print the book's quizzes and activities
- Access curriculum correlations
- Explore additional web applications that enhance the Lightbox experience

LIGHTBOX DIGITAL TITLES
Packed full of integrated media

VIDEOS

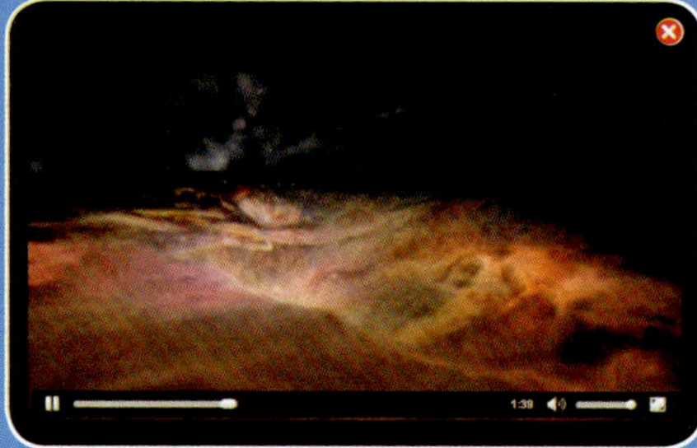

INTERACTIVE MAPS

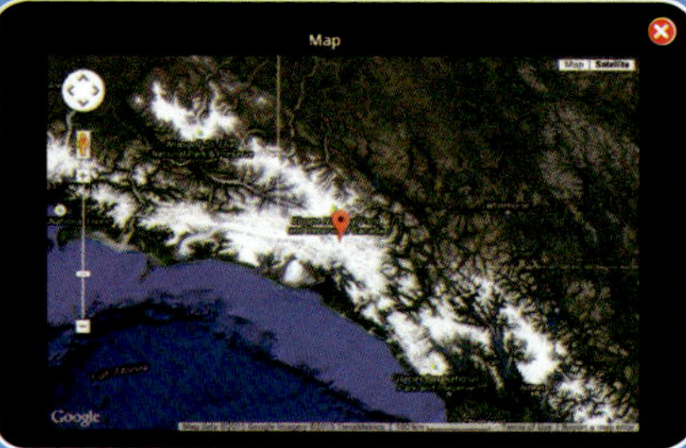

WEBLINKS

SLIDESHOWS

QUIZZES

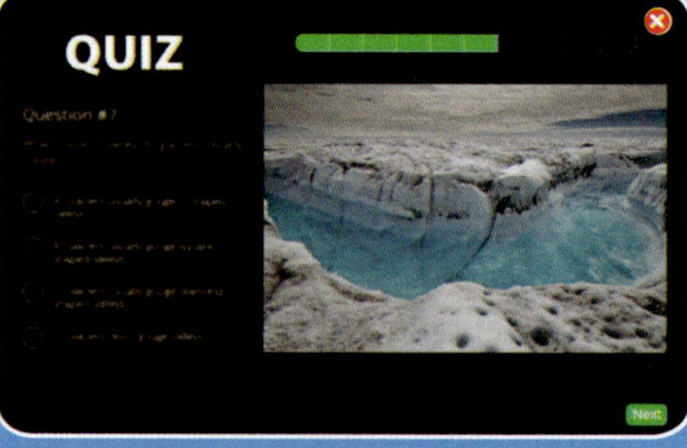

OPTIMIZED FOR

- ✓ TABLETS
- ✓ WHITEBOARDS
- ✓ COMPUTERS
- ✓ AND MUCH MORE!

Published by Smartbook Media Inc.
350 5th Avenue, 59th Floor New York, NY 10118
Website: www.openlightbox.com

Library of Congress Cataloging-in-Publication Data
Names: Weber, Valerie, author. | Gillespie, Katie, author.
Title: Fahrenheit 451 / Valerie Weber and Katie Gillespie.
Description: New York, NY : Smartbook Media Inc., [2019] | Series: Lightbox literature studies | Includes index.
Identifiers: LCCN 2018000594 (print) | LCCN 2018000723 (ebook) | ISBN 9781510536937 (Multi-Use eBook) | ISBN 9781510536920 (hard cover : alk. paper)
Subjects: LCSH: Bradbury, Ray, 1920-2012. Fahrenheit 451--Examinations--Study guides. | Book burning in literature. | Censorship in literature.
Classification: LCC PS3503.R167 (ebook) | LCC PS3503.R167 F339 2019 (print) | DDC 813/.54--dc23
LC record available at https://lccn.loc.gov/2018000594

Printed in Brainerd, Minnesota, United States
1 2 3 4 5 6 7 8 9 0 22 21 20 19 18

062018
121017

Editor: Katie Gillespie
Art Director: Terry Paulhus

The publisher acknowledges Getty Images, iStock, Alamy, and Wikimedia Commons as its primary image suppliers for this title.